# The Development of Federal Indian Law

Victoria Sutton, MPA, PhD, JD

American Indian Legal History Series

VARGAS PUBLISHING



ISBN- 978-1-7364743-3-4

Manufactured in the United States of America
First printing, 2026

Published and distributed by
Vargas Publishing
P.O. Box 6801
Lubbock, TX 79466
http://vargaspublishing.com

## Table of Contents

*Dedicated to*

*my American Indian ancestors and those first documented by America:*

*Elizabeth Cullom, Elizabeth Wooten, William Godwin, William Taylor* and She-La Bird

# Introduction

This book explores the foundations of American Indian Law and specifically, federal Indian Law in context with historical events that shaped and led to the development of federal Indian law. An examination of the text of U.S. Supreme Court opinions is necessary to appreciate the context and foundation of today's federal Indian law opinions.

Your first thoughts upon an initial reading of the first U.S. Supreme Court cases on Indian law, may be that surely these cases are no longer relevant or no longer law given the language and biases in the text? They are. The views are those that we today, must learn to interpret and apply to new cases. Your next thought might be, then why do we not just unravel all of these cases and invalidate their holdings and start over? While that kind of action is counter to our conservative and incremental way of shaping law, even if it were possible, it would undo commitments, policies, treaties and law that tribes as well as anyone interacting with tribes have come to rely on in investing time, resources and their future. More critical for the United States is that it would invalidate all the land transactions that put the title of aboriginal and Indian lands into the hands of the American government, so that titles could be given to settlers, and also to settle land claims with Indian Nations.

Questions like: Who is an Indian? What is an Indian tribe? How can tribes have sovereignty, yet be a dependent nation within the geographic boundaries of the United States are questions we explore in this book.

The book begins with the historical encounters with the Spanish, French and English colonists and explorers that shaped the treaties and laws that would create a framework for federal Indian law. Then Indian Tribes had relationships with colonies and states before federal law preempted state law. Opinions of the U.S. Supreme Court and other federal courts are reviewed in landmark cases, important to Federal Indian law today. Perspectives of tribes and some of the background for these cases is provided which is often complex and includes histories not covered in traditional courses.

Legal history of the Indigenous peoples of the United States influences every new problem in Indian Country that arises for resolution before a court of law, today. Legal documents from before the ratification of the United States Constitution, are also often binding and controlling in many issues.

## Chapter 1

## In the Pursuit of Land

Europeans, Asians and Scandinavians are all said to have set foot or seen the Americas as much as 500 years before Christopher Columbus, perhaps they were also looking for land or riches. However, the first recorded impact of enslaving Indians begins the impact of discovery starting with Christopher Columbus. Not only were Indians enslaved as part of exploring for gold, but they were also sent to Spain to be sold.

Maybe more impactful than the gold, Columbus sought was a gift he received from the Indians. On Oct 12, 1492, Christopher Columbus set foot on a Caribbean Island in the Bahamas (probably Hispanola) and was greeted by the Arawaks. They presented him with a gift of dried leaves which was tobacco.

The British were most likely first exposed to the use of tobacco in 1565 when a British Explorer brought some back from a voyage to Florida [National Park Service].

Soon thereafter, the first shipment of tobacco launched the tobacco market in England in 1610. This tobacco was grown in Spanish Colonial America and shipped to Spain. In 1612, John Rolfe returned from Trinidad where obtained "Spanish" tobacco seeds Nicotiana Tabacum from the Orinoco River. He obtained these seeds using questionable means from a ship captain. Rolfe wanted to cultivate this sweeter variety of tobacco in Virginia. Learning from the Powhatan Confederacy to cultivate Virginia tobacco, Rolfe believed he could grow the sweeter tobacco using the same methods in the Virginia climate.

The colonists had been introduced to tobacco by Native Americans, probably the Pamunkey Tribe. The Pamunkey used tobacco during ceremonies and considered it a sacred plant. It was not used recreationally. However, John Rolfe was an avid smoker.

The Navigation Laws, reenacted in 1660, specified "enumerated" colonial products that could only be shipped directly to England, Ireland or another English colony [Britannica].

John Rolfe's experiment was a success. This was followed by his marriage to Pocahontas married Rolfe, April 1, 1614[National Park Service]. His successful experiment came at a time the Virginia Colony was close to collapse. In the Virginia Colony in 1616, there were only six settlements and 351 settlers which was less than half the number five years earlier [Horn, James].

Pocahontas and John Rolfe traveled to England, and just after disembarking on a ship to return to the Virginia Colony in March 1617, Pocahontas died suddenly in Gravesend on this ship that was traveling back to Jamestown. Rolfe buried his wife and left their son with a relative and returned to Virginia to continue his tobacco trade.[5] It was upon his return that the failing Virginia colony began to give land grants away to individuals and societies of "adventurers" made up of financiers and merchants. The objective was to secure agricultural land and to cultivate tobacco. Anyone with a few acres could grow tobacco in what became a tobacco boom, saving the Virginia colony from demise.

During this period, John Rolfe, who served as secretary of state from 1614 to 1619, conducted the agricultural experiments that resulted in the development of a palatable and highly marketable strain of tobacco. It became the colonists' money crop, which fueled the spread of settlement and drove the Natives from their land [National Park Service].

Not only did this explosion in agriculture of tobacco drive the coastal Virginia Tribes from their land, but it also brought the demand for slaves to cultivate the labor intensive tobacco crop. The tobacco trade inspired and brought on the drive to bring slavery to America.

Meanwhile, the population of the Virginia Colony quickly increased from 351 in 1616 to slightly less than a thousand by early 1620.[Horn, James, p. 177]. The rapid increase in settlement and the wholesale stealing of land was enough to cause the Pamunkey Tribe to seek to expel the settlers. By 1622, the largest massacre against the settlers at that time, in the colonies was strategically planned and executed by Pamunkey Chief Opechancanough, killing about 20% of the colonists in America, [Horn, James, p. 189] in response to this rapid growth due to the tobacco market.

**Slavery as a commodity and a strategy**

That Native Americans did not make very good slaves made little difference in the commerce of slavery in early colonial America.

The enslavement of indigenous peoples of the Americas is part of our history that is not well known. Two books that attempted to shed light on this history won book awards in 2003, *The Indian Slave Trade: The Rise of the English Empire in the American South, 1670-1772* and in 2017, *The Other Slavery: The uncovered story of Indian enslavement in America.* The beginnings of the slave trade arose first in areas colonized by Spain — the southwest and the southeast U.S., beginning with Christopher Columbus's kidnapping of about 500 Taino people from the Caribbean to be enslaved in Europe. The Spanish enslaved Indigenous peoples through systems like the encomienda and repartimiento,4 which gave settlers the right to a certain portion of land and Indigenous people as slaves. The British soon found it useful to replace a dwindling fur trade. By 1772, every British colony had Indian slaves.5 It also means that these Native Nations from these regions share this history which other Native Nations in America do not, and may be unaware how devastating it was.

Slavery killed and removed more Native Americans than epidemics and diseases, contrary to generally believed history. But for the courage of a few priests, traders and enslaved captives, little would be known about it, according to the author.

Native American (Pequots, Narragansetts, Wampanoags a [Fisher, Linford D ] (and others) were told during King Phillips War (1675-76), that they should surrender to bring peace, and once they surrendered they were enslaved and sold. Most feared, was that they were going to be sent abroad to Bermuda, the Azore Islands (Portugal), Jamaica, Spain and Tangier in North Africa. [Fisher, Linford D ] Tens of thousands of Indian slaves went to Europe through the Azore Islands on their way to Europe.

Native American slavery "is a piece of the history of slavery that has been glossed over," Fisher said. "Between 1492 and 1880, between 2 and 5.5 million Native Americans were enslaved in the Americas in addition to 12.5 million African slaves." [Fisher, Linford D].

In *The Rediscovery of America: Native Peoples and the Unmaking of US History* (2024), Ned Blackhawk found that "nearly a million Native Americans were enslaved across the Americas in the sixteenth and seventeenth centuries and sent east across the Atlantic, many from Boston and Charleston. In the latter port, it was not until 1715 that more enslaved Africans from West Africa were imported than enslaved Indigenous people were exported."[Blackhawk, Ned].

Enslavement of Indigenous peoples started with Columbus in his famous 1492 arrival in the Americas, when he took about 500 slaves back to Europe. In fact, each group of colonists had their colonization methods: the English prioritized trade and trade relationships; the French prioritized relationships by intermarrying with Native people as much as possible; and the Spanish were known for using enslavement of Native people in their quests for gold and all the hard labor that entails those missions.

Spanish colonized the Southwest and the Southeastern U.S., leaving their names and their permanent damage from slavery. The English in New England enslaved Pequot people. Later, the English would continue the tradition of enslavement of Native peoples by land owners. Realizing that enslavement was not diplomatically helping the cause of the colonies, most prohibited the enslavement of Indigenous Americans by the mid-eighteenth century.

**A Short Legal History of Indian Slavery in Virginia**

In a case styled, *Robin v. Hardaway* (1772), in the General Court of Virginia, the highest court in the colony, held that Indian enslavement through the 17th Century had been illegal. [Ablovsky, G.] Virginia passed a law in 1691 making Indian slavery illegal. [Ablavsky, G.] George Mason, represented Robin, an enslaved Native American and eleven other plaintiffs. The plaintiffs were freed and their owners were ordered to pay nominal damages. The opinion was landmark in that it was the first Anglo-American court to find that if your mother was Indian then you could not be legally enslaved, the principle of *partus sequitur ventrem*. This led to many freedom suits throughout Virginia.

In 1804, a well-documented case, *Charles Evans and others vs. Lew*is *B. Allen* in a Lynchburg, Virginia court, established the requirements for freedom with a geneaology chart. [Library of Virginia].

In 1806, the Virginia Court of Appeals, the highest court in the state, took up the issue of Indian slavery. In the landmark decision, *Hudgins v. Wright,* the court considered whether the plaintiff the Virginia court affirmed that enslaving Indians had been illegal since the legislature in 1705 declared it illegal.

Courts in Connecticut, Louisiana, Missouri, New Jersey, South Carolina, and Tennessee all followed with legislatures and courts arguing about Virginia's cases that followed Robin, and whether descent from an American Indian mother was all that was required to defeat a claim of enslavement. [Ablavsky, G.].

**Descendants of Enslaved Indians**

Geneaologies of enslaved peoples are particularly difficult to build with official documents when only first names are used, and exportations, human sales and movements are undocumented or lost. DNA has provided a new pathway to determining ancestry along with traditional geneaology. Stories and traditions from Tribes can also connect the past with the present.

A group of geneaologists and descendants of an enslaved Native American from Isle of Wight, Virginia, citizen of the Cheraw or Saponi Tribe was connected using DNA to the descendants of a returning envoy from Azore

Islands, Portugal in the 1600s to known Saponi descendants. In a rare case where geneaologies could be constructed enough to establish why this ancestor returned to the Cheraw and Saponi community of Virginia. This can also explain a centuries old "mystery" of why many Virginia and North Carolina Indians said they were "Portuguese". It was thought by government and courts that it was untrue and simply used to avoid the application of "people of color" statutes that prevented many civil rights and freedoms enjoyed by the non-people of color population. But this may have cracked that once solid conclusion that it was a lie to avoid the law — these Native Americans were actually Portuguese as their nationality, but their race or ethnicity was Native American at least in part.

Today, St. David's Island is home to descendants of Indian slaves taken from the Pequot, Narragansett, Nipmuk and other Tribes in New England, and shipped away to Bermuda for profit and to take their land. [St George's Crown] They have re-connected with several of their ancestral tribes with ceremonies and new bonds among the families.

**Reflecting on this period**

Native American slavery made much more of an impact in terms of scope, numbers of enslaved Native Americans and the consequences of the loss of people and land than perhaps acknowledged or even understood. More research, award-winning books and DNA studies can provide a better picture of an early history that we should not forget.

in order to convert them to Christianity, which was a job expected of Spain by the Catholic Church.

But how did Vitoria reason that Spain could ultimately claim the lands? First, Vitoria concluded that the Indians were not suited for the administration of government which brought civility and control over life. If Spain could provide this government — for their benefit of course — then this would in effect allow Spain to control the land. This laid the foundation for the understanding of the trust relationship between the federal government and Indians in modern American Indian law. Second, Vitoria reasoned that under a natural law theory, that Indians had obligations as well as rights, which allowed visitors, travelers, traders and churches on their missions to convert. Should the indigenous peoples resist this obligation, then the Spanish would be morally justified, under a just war theory, to fight and conquer the Indians. Thus, the foundation for the conquerers's right to possession of the land. Because of the rights held by Indians, the use of treaties was seen as a way to gain the consent of the indigenous peoples with the domination of the colonizers.
[from S. James Anaya, Indigenous Peoples in International Law 2d ed. Oxford Press 2004].

The failure of Spain to heed the advice of Vitoria, in respecting the land and rights of the indigenous people led to the Pueblo Revolt of 1620. A landmark event for the Pueblo people, the harsh rule of the Spanish and Mexicans was turned back after more than one hundred years of colonization aggression. This event is a pivotal landmark in Pueblo government and history, and the events which surrounded the Pueblo Revolt of 1620 are important in today's governance among the Pueblo people.

**Treaty Period**

There are many treaties with tribes with nations that did not win the colonizing war. Treaties with tribes on the East Coast of the U.S. were made with Switzerland (where New Bern, North Carolina is, today). There are treaties between tribes and Spain in those historically colonized areas of Florida, Texas and California (the Treaty of Guadalupe Hidalgo, for example).

One of the early treaties, The Treaty of Middle Plantation 1677, was made between the Indians of Virginia and the Colony of Virginia. Upon Virginia entering the United States, the treaties and agreements made by the colony were assumed by the new Commonwealth of Virginia.

The Treaty of Middle Plantation began with a recognition of the sovereignty of King Charles II, by the paying of tribute by the Indians to the King. This paying of tribute has been a continuous practice for more than three hundred years, based on the Treaty of Middle Plantation, when all of the Virginia tribes come to pay tribute to the Governor of Virginia, bringing venison (deer meat), fish or turkeys.

**The Treaty of Middle Plantation 1677**

ARTICLES OF PEACE
Between
The Most Serene and Mighty PRINCE
CHARLES II.
By the the Grace of God,
King of England, Scotland, France and Ireland,
Defender of the Faith, &c.
And several
Indian Kings and Queens &c.
Concluded the 29th day of May, 1677.

PUBLISHED BY HIS MAJESTIES COMMAND

LONDON,

Wife of Gov. Davis accepts the tribute in 1919.

Pamunkey Chief, Tecumseh D. Cook, delivering tribute to Gov. Allmond in 1959.

Virginia tribes paying tribute to Gov. McAuliffe (2012). Evanne Armour/Nexstar Capitol Bureau

The second and third articles, reproduced below, set forth the way in which the Indians would hold their land, agreeing never to disturb their ownership, as long as they remained loyal to the English. The twenty-two articles of the Treaty, set forth other agreements that Indians would continue to govern within their existing tribal nations, that they can travel and hunt (as long as they obtain a permit), relations with other tribes, translators, and negotiating differences rather than going to war.

---

> *II. That thereupon the said Indian Kings & Queens and their Subjects shall hold their lands, and have the same confirmed to them and their posterity by Patent under the Seale of this his Magesties Colony, without any fee gratuity or Reward for ye same, in such sort, and in as free and firme manner as others his Magesties Liege Subjects, have and enjoye their Lands, and possessions, paying onely yearly for, and in Liew of a Quitrent or acknowledgement for the same three Indian Arrowes.*
>
> *III. That all Indians who are in amity with us, & have not land siffitient to plant up, be upon information forthwith provided for, and land laid out, and confirmed to them as affores'd never to be disturbed therein, or taken from them, soe long as they owne keep and maintaine the due obedience & Subjection to his Majestie his Govern'r and Government; & amity & friendship towards the English.*

---

The policy of colonization, typified by this Treaty expresses more humility by the colonists as they seek the good favor of the tribal Nations to assist them in their colonizing efforts. Article IV of the Treaty gives us a sense of apology and diplomacy from the English for causing the Indians to retaliate for wrongs done to them by the English:

> *IV. Whereas by the mutuall discontents, Complaints, jealousies, and feares of English and Indians occasioned by the violent intrusions of divers English into their lands, forceing the Indians by way of Revenge, to kill the Cattle & hoggs of the English, whereby offence, and injuries being given, and done on boeth sides, the peace of this his Majesties Colony hath bin much disturbed, and the late unhappy Rebellion by this means in a great measure begunne & fomented which hath involved this Country into soe much Ruine, & misery, for prevention of which injuries and evill consequences as much as possible we may for time to come it is hereby concluded and enacted that noe English, shall seate or plant nearer then three miles of any Indian towne . . .*

---

A period of treatymaking brought dozens of agreements along the eastern seaboard between tribes and colonies that were needed for their efforts at colonization and prioritizing trade:

1679 - Albany Conference (permitted Iroquois to hunt and

travel through Manahoac lands, blocked Algonquian tribes in Tidewater from Piedmont)

1684 - Albany treaty signed by Lord Howard (blocked English settlement in Iroquois-controlled Piedmont, restricting Northern Virginia occupation to Tidewater area)

1722 - Treaty of Albany (restricted Iroquois to west of the Blue Ridge)

1744 - Treaty of Lancaster (Iroquois sold Virginia their claims of lands "to the setting sun," pushing them out of Shenandoah Valley to west of the Alleghenies)

1748 - Virginia and Pennsylvania distribute gifts to Ohio River tribes at Logstown (part of competition with French traders)

1752 - Treaty of Logstown (limited Delaware and Shawnee claims south of the Ohio River)

1768 - Treaties of Fort Stanwix and Hard Labor

1770 - Treaty of Lochaber (ceding title to the lands north of the Ohio River to the English)

1775 - Treaty of Sycamore Shoals (limited Cherokee claims in far Southwestern Virginia)

1777 - Treaty of Long Island (limited Cherokee claims in far Southwestern Virginia)

The next major treaty was the Treaty of Hopewell

with the Cherokee Tribe, November 28th, 1785, 7 Stat. 18, which established the frontier boundary and opened a floodgate of new settlement in Virginia and North Carolina.

During this period, the Trade Wars were brought on by the lack of a cohesive national policy of promoting free trade between the colonies and the tribes, due to the proprietary nature of the colonies. The Trade Wars in Virginia and the Carolinas were fiercely carried on, at the highest levels of their governments. In 1698, the South Carolina House of Commons proposed legislation to forbid Virginia traders to trade with any South Carolina Indian. That bill failed along with a 1701 legislative proposal that goods of all Virginia traders be confiscated when in South Carolina. However, a bill to tax horses being brought from Virginia into South Carolina did pass. The stated purpose was "Care be taken to bring the Catawba Indians more dependient on this Goverment: by discourageing the Virginia tradeing among them."

Virginians, however despite the law, continued to trade with the Indians of South Carolina, and on June 13, 1707, the South Carolina Commons House recommended to the Governor that he seize the Virginia Indian traders, "if it may be done by the Laws of England." The House was not sure if this was legal, but determined that a 1703 Act which required an export duty of three pence on every deerskin and beaver skin taken out of the colony provided for arrest of violators. So, in 1707, the Carolina government invoked the law and confiscated the pelts of a Virginia trader who had left his pelts in a Catawba town for safekeeping.

The Virginia trader immediately petitioned the Commons House for redress, but was told it was not in their jurisdiction to decide. Later, the Board of Trade and

Plantations wrote a letter to the lord proprietors of the South Carolina colony asking whether the seizure was "done by virtue of any orders from Your Lordships and upon what grounds . . ."

A year later, the Lord Proprietors responded in a letter that the seizure was for the failure of the Virginians to pay the export levies on the pelts, but that there was no law to forbid their trading in South Carolina. The Virginia traders then went to the Colonial Council in Williamsburg which was the seat of power in the colonies, April 28, 1708. The traders were able to get some of their goods returned, but were prohibited from crossing into South Carolina in the future. The open trade wars began.

The Virginia Colonial Council wrote the Governor of South Carolina saying that:

> *. . . this manner of proceeding is althogether new and unprecedented that her Majesty first by her royall instructions granted and afterwards confirmed by Law a free trade to all the inhabitants of this Coilony with all Indians watsoever . . . therefore the Government of South Carolina hav no authority to monopolize all the Indian trade.*

The Virginia Council then issued passports to its traders.

The matter was taken to Queen Anne, who responded on September 26, 1709, but her letter did not arrive until April 1710, and said that she decreed that the Virginians be permitted to trade freely with the "Western Indians" without interference from South Carolina." South Carolina continued to place burdens on the traders, and began requiring that they travel to Charleston to get permits to trade with the Indians — a trip of at least a couple hundred miles out of the way of the trading path. Finally, even those Virginians who obtained permits were questioned and their goods were confiscated. Queen Anne and the Privy Council acted in January 1713, to disallow the action taken by the South Carolinians, taking another year to arrive in the colonies. [Excerpted from Douglas Summers Brown, *The Catawba Indians, The People of the River*, 110-114 (1966)]

Native Americans were essential to the success of these propriety colonies and so honoring treaties and encouraging peace was a priority for the colonists. Religion also continued to be important with Christianization of Indians continuing as a mission for the colonists, in some ways, justifying their taking their land. As Justice Marshall wrote, *The potentates of the old world found no difficulty in convincing themselves that they made ample compensation to the inhabitants of the new by bestowing on them civilization and Christianity . . . [Johnson v. M'Intosh (1823)].*

**Confederation (1776-1788)**

During this period of time, the Articles of Confederation were written, which addressed the important trade issues with Indians and Indian tribal nations. The Indian nations were in a strong political position with the United States, which had just declared its independence from Great Britain. Alliances with other Nations on the part of Indian tribes led to the need to use treaties to gain trust and certainty with the Indian Nations.

**Trade and Intercourse Period (1789-1835)**

It was the trade wars among the colonies, like those described above, which led to the discussion at the Constitutional Convention that a mere amendment to the Articles of Confederation would not cure these trade war problems. Influenced primarily by the trade with the Indians and the trade wars, the Constitutional Convention determined that a commerce clause must be written in a new Constitution, because this omission made the Articles of Confederation unworkable. This led to what is called the Indian Commerce Clause, and is one of the three mentions of Indians as a race, in the United States Constitution.

The U.S. Constitution was written and ratified in 1789, and the importance of the relationship with Indians and Indian Nations is evident. Indians are the only race specifically mentioned in the U.S. Constitution, and they are mentioned three times. The Indian Commerce Clause states that the federal government will have control over trade and commerce with the Indians.

This critical time laid the foundation for land ownership and trade issues with the Indians and Indian Nations. The Trade and Intercourse Act was passed in 1789 and 1791 (25 U.S.C. §177), gave control over land purchases from Indians and trade with the Indians to the new federal government, and prohibited individuals and states from buying land from Indians. Prior to this, individuals may have been prohibited from buying land from Indians by their state laws, but states were continuing to buy land from Indians. The reason for the control over trade was because the states had created a series of "trade wars" between themselves in order to keep commerce within their borders, essentially stopping the free flow of commerce which would be essential to the building of a new nation.

Thomas Jefferson reflected on the rights of American Indians to their property when he confessed that natural rights were not applied to the actions of the Europeans in taking lands from American Indians:

> *[W]hoever shall attempt to trace the claims of the European nations to the countrys [sic] in America from the principles of Justice, or reconcile the invasions made on the Native Indians to the natural rights of mankind, will find that he is pursuing a Chimera, which exists only in his own imagination, against the evidence of indisputable facts.*

[Wilcomb E. Washburn, *The Moral and Legal Justifications for Dispossessing the Indians, in* Seventeenth Century America: Essays on Colonial History 15, 26 (James M. Smith ed., 1959)].

**Removal Period (1835-1861)**

After the War of 1812, conciliatory attitudes changed, and the Indian Nations were not in a strong political position now that the threat of Great Britain had subsided. President Andrew Jackson was elected in 1830, and instituted the policy of "removal" of Indians to make way for settlement based on the grand notion of "manifest destiny", a term which was repeated in Justice Marshall's foundation trilogy of cases, although it had no legal meaning. It was an idea that white colonists were entitled to sweep across the continent taking whatever they found along the way because it was their "destiny."

Efforts to make treaties with tribes turned into

coercive actions and existing treaties were amended or ignored as settlement pushed westward. Often the representatives of the Tribes who signed the treaties were not the leaders or chiefs of the Tribes, but it was sufficient for the U.S. Senate to find that it could be ratified. The policy became one of divide and conquer, and tribes were forceably removed and marched on foot and wagon to "Indian Country" during all kinds of weather resulting in the genocide of unknown numbers of Native Americans. "Indian country" was an area that today is a large part the State of Oklahoma, and parts of the State of Kansas. Thanks to a recent U.S. Supreme Court decision [*McGirt v. Oklahoma*, 591 U.S. ___ , 140 S. Ct. 2452 (2020)], it was recognized that one of these reservations was never actually extinguished and by extension all other reservations in the state of Oklahoma were never extinguished. It was a landmark case that was a criminal jurisdictional case that turned out to have far reaching consequences. Again, the conflict of one individual resulted in a decision that affected all of Indian Country and multiple tribal nations and their treaty interpretations.

Also during the 1830s, the first American Indian scholar, William Apes, wrote "On Our Own Ground," challenging the massive land acquisitions in Connecticut. Eventually tribal nations in New York were able to establish illegal land transfers by the state of New York that violated the federal 1790 Trade and Intercourse Act, resulting in the confirmation of their reservation. [*County of Oneida v. Oneida Indian Nation of New York State*, 470 U.S. 226 (1985)].

**Reservation Period (1861-1887)**

The U.S. Civil War from 1860 to 1864 led to divisions among the Indian Nations. The Western Cherokee sided with the North, while the Southern Cherokee sided with the Southern Confederacy. The Southern Cherokee made a treaty with the Confederacy which granted them a seat in Congress as well as other concessions which would give them a greater influence over their government.

The reservation period set up boundaries for Native Nations and rules for being confined within those boundaries.

During this period the Indian Wars on the frontier provided a new assignment for troops trained in the U.S. Civil War. Western scouts were recruited from among the Indian Tribes and they were trained as members of the U.S. Army. Conflicts, hangings and open calls to shoot Indians continued to be the policy of the West.

In 1871, the U.S. Congress, having grown tired of the expenses of reservations, ended the treaty-making power of the U.S. President. Arguably an unconstitutional Act, there was no one who wanted to oppose it, so it is still law.

The Courts of Federal Offences were created in 1883 and affirmed by the federal court in 1888, setting up a system of controlling crimes and criminal enforcement on Indian lands, taking away tribal governmental control of offenders.

**The Allotment and Assimilation Era (1887 - 1934)**

Allotments authorized by the Dawes Act began implementing an assimilation policy that would cause destruction to Indian people, their culture, language and governance, by breaking up their land held in common, and allotting small lots to individual tribal members. This assumed that these tribal members would be farmers and would use their land as farms, where the women of the families were the farmers and the men were the hunters, leaving the men with no role in this new American policy for assimilation.

Residential schools were also created as another strategy for assimilation. "Kill the Indian, and save the man" was the slogan for these schools that were mostly run by religious organizations and churches in conjunction with the federal government. Often, these children were snatched from reservations and torn from their families against their wishes, without parent consent. These children were often told their parents did not want them or that they were dead. The survivors of these residential schools are speaking out about their experiences.

**Indian Reorganization Act (1934-1940)**

The Indian Reorganization Act (IRA) was intended to replace Indian Tribe structure and take a standardized constitution. Indian tribes were required to hold elections as to whether to accept the new constitution and if they decided not to accept the constitution, then they would be terminated as a federally recognized tribe.

**Termination (1940-1962)**

Having failed to assimilate Indians, and deciding to simply end all treaty obligations, Pres. Eisenhower led the Termination era. With no real plan, the federal government ordered Indians to leave reservations, put them on buses and trains and dropped them off in major metropolitan areas, with no resources, jobs or support structure. This inspired the organization of the American Indian Movement (AIM) and resistance to forced destruction of tribal structure and culture by reclaiming land. The Occupation of Alcatraz was a major demonstration of the strength of the Indians in America who wanted autonomy. A "Proclamation for the Indian Occupation of Alcatraz," was written by Adam Fortunate Eagle and the United Bay Area Council of American Indians during the occupation of Alcatraz Island (1969-1971).

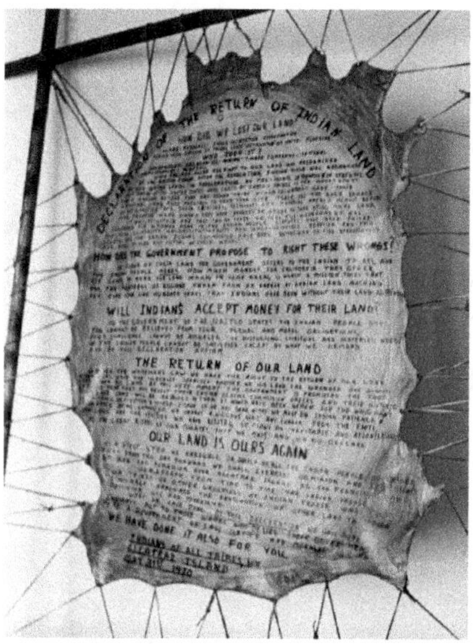


Photo credit: NPS and Ilka Hartmann

The occupation of Alcatraz was to reclaim land once owned by Tribes but now unused and owned by the federal government. Alcatraz Island fit that description.

Many Indian tribes were terminated during this era, and many were never reestablished. Many, however, fought to continue as Tribes and to be reestablished, years later.

## Self-Determination (1962 - present)

The Self-Determination Period was ushered in by President Nixon, who wanted to return self-governance to Indian Tribes. A resurgence in a return to culture, language and tribal governance has come from the federal policy giving Tribes greater autonomy.

The Indian Child Welfare Act (ICWA) was passed in 1978 to allow control over the future of the Tribe to be returned to Indian Tribes, through their participation in Indian custody and adoption proceedings. The Indian Gaming and Regulatory Act (IGRA) of 1988 was passed to provide a space with legal authority for negotiations between states and Indian tribes for the establishment of gaming establishments. Both of these major statutes create increased autonomy for Indian Tribes.

## Chapter 3

## The Marshall Trilogy

The United States Supreme Court, the third branch of the new federal government, was established with its first Chief Justice John Jay. But it was not until the second Chief Justice, John Marshall, was appointed, that the Court addressed the legal relationship between Indian nations and the United States.

Justice John Marshall was born in southwestern Virginia on the frontier, and it is certain he had encounters with the Overhill Cherokees, many other tribes that traveled down the Appalachian Mountain ridges, and settlement or "parched corn" Indians who assimilated into towns and villages. He served in Gen. Washington's Army, and was part of the notorious battle where Gen. Lee retreated against the orders of Gen. Washington. He rose in the ranks to become an Associate Judge Advocate of the U.S. Army, and participated in the trial of Benedict Arnold. He was also distantly related to Thomas Jefferson, also of Virginia. He was steeped in the visceral role of founding the United States, and now he was critical to interpreting the key document that would direct the moral and legal direction of the new nation. How he interpreted the embattled history of the colonists relationship with the tribal nations in the context of their status in the U.S. Constitution would form the foundation cases that influence all of federal Indian Law. [Beveridge, Albert J.].

Tribal nations were specifically named as a third sovereign in the U.S. Constitution in the Commerce Clause, and that would ensure the continuity of their own self-determination.

The first judicial opinion of the Marshall trilogy in resolving a land ownership dispute, established how the U.S. reasoned that they had good title in acquiring the land from Indian Nations. The second opinions, known as the Cherokee cases, were about building a judicially cognizable justification for taking tribal and aboriginal land in exchange for allowing the continued existence and self-governance of tribes as sovereign bodies. Defining what that sovereignty meant within the boundaries of another sovereign nation was the task undertaken by Justice Marshall in these opinions.

## Examining the Marshall Trilogy

The federal Indian law foundation cases — referred to as the Marshall Trilogy, establish the legal relationship between tribes and the United States in the context of the U.S. Constitution. These cases, written by Chief Justice John Marshall, define the way federal Indian law cases are decided and interpreted to resolve land and self-governance issues, today.

The first of these judicial decisions that provided the foundation for all subsequent federal Indian law in the United States was decided by the U.S. Supreme Court in 1823 in a case called ***Johnson v. McIntosh*** .[1] This opinion established that land grants made by tribal chiefs to individuals from 1773 to 1775 — prior to the establishment of the United States— were valid. Basing this decision on the "right of occupancy", at the sufferance of the United States, the court held that Indians *did* have rights to convey. (To find

[1] *Johnson v. McIntosh*, 21 U.S. ( 8 Wheat.) 543 (1823).

otherwise, would have been to invalidate treaties which gave immense tracts of land to the colonial and U.S. governments.) The court further established that the "doctrine of discovery" and "title by conquer," had evolved into the current system of controlling land of the tribes which had been conquered. Chief Justice John Marshall wrote in *Johnson v. McIntosh*, 21 U.S. (8 Wheat.) 543 (1823), that whatever the "original justice of the claim," and however "opposed to natural right, and to the usages of civilized nations," he was constrained in doing justice for Indian peoples because he sat in the "Courts of the conqueror." Establishing title in the sovereign was possible with some restraints, "when the conquest is complete, and the conquered inhabitants can be blended with the conquerors, or safely governed as a distinct people."[2]

Further, Justice Marshall found that taking land was a considered a righteous bargain because the Indians received Christianity for their land. He wrote:

> *The potentates of the old world found no difficulty in convincing themselves that they made ample compensation to the inhabitants of the new by bestowing on them civilization and Christianity in exchange for unlimited independence.* [*Johnson v. McIntosh*, 21 U.S. (8 Wheat.) 543, 573 (1823)]

The following excerpt of that case, explains the court's reasoning as to how the United States could hold a valid title to the land that had been occupied by Indigenous peoples in the United States.

---

[2] *Johnson v. McIntosh,* 21 U.S. ( 8 Wheat.) 543 (1823).

## *Johnson and Graham's Lessee v. M'Intosh*

Supreme Court of the United States
21 U.S. 543 (Feb 28, 1823)

Conquest gives a title which the Courts of the conqueror cannot deny, whatever the private and speculative opinions of individuals may be, respecting the original justice of the claim which has been successfully asserted. The British government, which was then our government, and whose rights have passed to the United States, asserted a title to all the lands occupied by Indians, within the chartered limits of the British colonies. It asserted also a limited sovereignty over them, and the exclusive right of extinguishing the title which occupancy gave to them. These claims have been maintained and established as far west as the river Mississippi, by the sword. The title to a vast portion of the lands we now hold, originates in them. It is not for the Courts of this country to question the validity of this title, or to sustain one which is incompatible with it. . . .

The title by conquest is acquired and maintained by force. The conqueror prescribes its limits. Humanity, however, acting on public opinion, has established, as a general rule, that the conquered shall not be wantonly oppressed, and that their condition shall remain as eligible as is compatible with the objects of the conquest. Most usually, they are incorporated with the victorious nation, and become subjects or citizens of the government with which they are connected. The new and old members of the society mingle with each other; the distinction between them is gradually lost, and they make one people. . . . When the conquest is complete, and the conquered inhabitants can be blended with the conquerors, or safely governed as a distinct people, public opinion, which not even the conqueror can disregard, imposes these restraints upon him; and he cannot neglect them without injury to his fame, and hazard to his power. But the tribes of Indians inhabiting this country were fierce savages, whose occupation was war, and whose subsistence was drawn chiefly from the forest. To leave them in possession of their country, was to leave the country a wilderness; to govern them as a distinct people, was impossible, because they were as brave and as high spirited as they were fierce, and were ready to repel by arms every attempt on their independence. What was the inevitable consequence of this state of things? The Europeans were under the necessity either of abandoning the country, and relinquishing their pompous claims to it, or of enforcing those claims by the sword, and by the adoption of principles adapted to the condition of a people with whom it was impossible to mix, and who could not be governed as a distinct society, or of remaining in their neighbourhood, and exposing themselves and their families to the perpetual hazard of being massacred. Frequent and bloody wars, in which the whites were not always the aggressors, unavoidably ensued. European policy, numbers, and skill, prevailed. As the white population advanced, that of the Indians necessarily receded. The country in the immediate neighbourhood of agriculturists became unfit for them. The game fled into thicker and more unbroken forests, and the Indians followed. The soil, to which the crown originally claimed title, being no longer occupied by its ancient inhabitants, was parcelled out according to the will of the sovereign power, and taken possession of by persons who claimed immediately from the crown, or mediately, through its grantees or deputies. That law which regulates, and ought to regulate in general, the relations between the conqueror and conquered, was incapable of application to a people under such circumstances. The resort to some new and different rule, better adapted to the actual state of things, was unavoidable. Every rule which can be suggested will be found to be attended with great difficulty. However extravagant the pretension of converting the discovery of an inhabited country into conquest may appear; if the principle has been asserted in the first instance, and afterwards sustained; if a country has been acquired and held under it; if the property of the great mass of the community originates in it, it becomes the law of the land, and cannot be questioned. So, too, with respect to the concomitant principle, that the Indian inhabitants are to be considered merely as occupants, to be protected, indeed, while in peace, in the possession of their lands, but to be deemed incapable of transferring the absolute title to others. However, this restriction may be opposed to natural right, and to the usages of civilized nations, yet, if it be indispensable to that system under which the country has been settled, and be adapted to the actual condition of the two people, it may, perhaps, be supported by reason, and certainly cannot be rejected by Courts of justice. The proclamation issued by the King of Great Britain, in 1763, has been considered, and, we think, with reason, as constituting an additional objection to the title of the plaintiffs. By that proclamation, the crown reserved under its own dominion and protection, for the use of the Indians, "all the land and territories lying to the westward of the sources of the rivers which fall into the sea from the west and northwest," and strictly forbade all British subjects from making any purchases or settlements whatever, or taking possession of the reserved lands. It has been contended, that, in this proclamation, the king transcended his constitutional powers; and the case of *Campbell v. Hall*, (reported by Cowper,) is relied on to support this position.It is supposed to be a principle of universal law, that, if an uninhabited country be discovered by a number of individuals, who acknowledge no connexion with, and owe no allegiance to, any government whatever, the country becomes the property of the discoverers, so far at least as they can use it. They acquire a title in common. The title of the whole land is in the whole society. It is to be divided and parcelled out according to the will of the society, expressed by the whole body, or by that organ which is authorized by the whole to express it.

If the discovery be made, and possession of the country be taken, under the authority of an existing government, which is acknowledged by the emigrants, it is supposed to be equally well settled, that the discovery is made for the whole nation, that the country becomes a part of the nation, and that the vacant soil is to be disposed of by that organ of the government which has the constitutional power to dispose of the national domains, by that organ in which all vacant territory is vested by law. According to the theory of the British constitution, all vacant lands are vested in the crown, as representing the nation; and the exclusive power to grant them is admitted to reside in the crown, as a branch of the royal prerogative. It has been already shown, that this principle was as fully recognised in America as in the island of Great Britain. All the lands we hold were originally granted by the crown; and the establishment of a regal government has never been considered as impairing its right to grant lands within the chartered limits of such colony. In addition to the proof of this principle, furnished by the immense grants, already mentioned, of lands lying within the chartered limits of Virginia, the continuing right of the crown to grant lands lying within that colony was always admitted. A title might be obtained, either by making an entry with the surveyor of a county, in pursuance of law, or by an order of the governor in council, who was the deputy of the king, or by an immediate grant from the crown. In Virginia, therefore, as well as elsewhere in the British dominions, the complete title of the crown to vacant lands was acknowledged. So far as respected the authority of the crown, no distinction was taken between vacant lands and lands occupied by the Indians. The title, subject only to the right of occupancy by the Indians, was admitted to be in the king, as was his right to grant that title. The lands, then, to which this proclamation referred, were lands which the king had a right to grant, or to reserve for the Indians. The authority of this proclamation, so far as it respected this continent, has never been denied, and the titles it gave to lands have always been sustained in our Courts. It has been stated, that in the memorial transmitted from the Cabinet of London to that of Versailles, during the controversy between the two nations, respecting boundary, which took place in 1755, the Indian right to the soil is recognised. But this recognition was made with reference to their character as Indians, and for the purpose of showing that they were fixed to a particular territory. It was made for the purpose of sustaining the claim of his Britannic majesty to dominion over them. . . It has never been contended, that the Indian title amounted to nothing. Their right of possession has never been questioned. The claim of government extends to the complete ultimate title, charged with this right of possession, and to the exclusive power of acquiring that right.

The object of the crown was to settle the seacoast of America; and when a portion of it was settled, without violating the rights of others, by persons professing their loyalty, and soliciting the royal sanction of an act, the consequences of which were ascertained to be beneficial, it would have been as unwise as ungracious to expel them from their habitations, because they had obtained the Indian title otherwise than through the agency of government.

Judgment affirmed, with costs.

---

The "memorial" referred to in the opinion between London and Versailles in 1755, was the French admonishing the English for attacking their ship without provocation and then the English failing to apologize and pay restitution, all tantamount to a declaration of war. Marshall references the 1755 memorial as the first official recognition of Indians in America and the right to their land. During this time the British were enticing Indians to withdraw from all relations

pleaſure. The buſineſs therefore of the Engliſh governors, at this congreſs, was to aſcertain the limits of the lands in diſpute, reconcile the Six Nations with their nephews the Delawares, remove every cauſe of miſunderſtanding between the Engliſh and the Indians, detach theſe ſavages entirely from the French intereſt, eſtabliſh a firm peace, and induce them to exert their influence in perſuading the Twightwees to accede to this treaty.

1755 Memorial between London and Versailles and supporting documentation

with the French due to their ongoing conflict. The English at the time recognized the "Indian right to the soil" by seeking to determine what lands were at stake occupied by the Indians.

By acknowledging the need to know the "limits of the land in dispute" with the Indians the British acknowledged the Indians dominion and control over the land and their right to occupy it. But the motive for the British is to defeat the French by conceding that the Indians own and control their land in order to reach agreement that they cease relations with the French.

While the acknowledgment of the Indians' "right to soil" is affirming and useful, the court's analysis uses two legal fictions to take control of the land, both diminishing sovereignty: the Indian Trust Doctrine and the "domestic dependent nations" analyses of sovereignty.

Chief Justice Marshall opens his opinion with "[C]onquest gives a title which the Courts of the conqueror cannot deny," that gives us an idea where the opinion will end – Indians' land interests will be subordinate to the U.S. land interests.

The affirming doctrine of the rights of Indians was stated in the negative, as ". . . [I]t has never been contended, that the Indian title amounted to nothing. Their right of possession has never been questioned."

What was at issue here was the title of a British citizen who had acquired his land from Indians, through the authority of the government. Without recognizing the Indians had a "right in soil" to transfer the land to the British citizen, the British citizen would hold nothing. This would extend to all of American land titles, that is, the land acquired through treaties with Indian tribes. If the court did not recognize

Indian title in this individual case, then the court could not recognize any of the treaty-acquired land was legally owned! Thus the tribes received just enough acknowledgment of their "right to soil" as was required to recognize the title that was passed to American non-Indian land title holders.

The history of the loss of land to tribes is told by Chief Justice Marshall with striking aloofness, as if he is unaware of the broken treaties, attacks on tribes, and decimating diseases brought from Europe that disposed Indians from their land.

> *The country in the immediate neighbourhood of agriculturists became unfit for them. The game fled into thicker and more unbroken forests, and the Indians followed. The soil, to which the crown originally claimed title, being no longer occupied by its ancient inhabitants, was parcelled out according to the will of the sovereign power, and taken possession of by persons who claimed immediately from the crown, or mediately, through its grantees or deputies.*

The tribes on the East coast met with genocidal government actions, including well-documented slavery that lasted a century; as well as intentional use of smallpox in blankets to "exterminate" Indians. During the Nineteenth Century, states used the legislature and the judiciary to fine Native landholders for "crimes" that required payment of fines in their land. Some of these crimes included anti-miscegenation crimes, and "tied-mule" cases. A Native farmer would find a mule a local or neighbor had tied to a tree on his property, followed immediately with the local sheriff arriving to arrest the Native farmer for theft of the mule. The fines for "people of color" (classification that included Native people) was forfeiture of land.

If these methods failed, the legislature could pass "settlement" acts. These are legislative dispositions of property conflicts that are not necessarily fair, but bring to closure the outstanding conflict, fair or not.

By 1790, the United States Congress passed the first federal law to stop the sale and trade of land between individuals, states and Native Americans or tribal nations. (The British has passed a similar law that had been in effect in America since ___). This first U.S. law was the 1790 Trade and Intercourse Act, and that gave the federal government exclusive control over the acquisition of Indian land through treatymaking.

---

# Chapter 4

## The Cherokee Cases

The Cherokee cases presented a major legal conflict between the sovereign Cherokee Nation centered in Georgia, and the state of Georgia, seeking to impose state law within the boundaries of the sovereign Cherokee Nation.

The next two cases in the trilogy involve the Cherokee Nation in Georgia in the 1830s, called the Cherokee cases. Both cases arise from the conflict over the arrest of a non-Indian minister who was being detained on questionable legal grounds. Like many American Indian law cases that followed, a case involving an individual often results in deciding a much broader legal issue that affects all tribes. That was certainly the outcome for these next two cases. Together they form the judicial interpretation for the doctrines of trust responsibility, the characterization of tribal nations as "domestic dependent nations", tribal sovereignty and the supremacy and binding nature of treaties.

### Examining the Cherokee Cases

In 1831 and 1832, two cases involving Cherokee Nation and Georgia state jurisdictional issues came before the U.S. Supreme Court. In the first case initiated by an Indian tribe, the Cherokees brought this case before the U.S. Supreme Court[3] as the court of original jurisdiction for resolving legal disputes between sovereigns. To achieve this kind of original jurisdiction in the U.S. Supreme Court, the

[3] *Cherokee Nation v. Georgia,* 30 U.S. (5 Pet.) 1 (1831).

Cherokee Nation had to be considered a "foreign nation" as defined in Art. III, § 2 of the U.S. Constitution. However, the Cherokee Nation lost their argument for jurisdiction, with Justice Marshall finding them to be "domestic dependent nations" although capable of self-government, but ***not*** a "foreign government".[4] This left the Cherokees with no judicial forum, since their dispute was with the state of Georgia, and represented a major blow to Indian tribal sovereignty.

Just one year later, the U.S. Supreme Court was faced with the second case, again, a conflict between the Cherokee Nation and Georgia, as to whether Georgia could extend the jurisdiction of its civil and criminal laws over the Cherokee Nation in ***Worcester v. Georgia***.[5] This issue was the one that had given rise to the Cherokee Nation's case, ***Cherokee Nation v. Georgia*** the previous year, but an issue that the court never reached because they decided the case on jurisdictional grounds ---- that the Cherokee Nation was not a foreign government and therefore could not litigate with a sovereign state in the U.S. Supreme Court under Art. III, § 2. This time, however, the United States Supreme Court found that the Cherokee Nation, while not a nation, *was* a sovereign, and Georgia therefore had no jurisdiction in the Cherokee Nation, although it was still within the boundaries of the state.

In 1830, President Andrew Jackson signed removal legislation that was intended to open lands in the

---

[4] U.S. Const., Art. III

[5] In ***Worcester***, a missionary to the Cherokee Nation was appealing a criminal conviction by the state of Georgia. On this occasion, the U.S. Supreme Court simply could not avoid deciding the issue.

southeastern United States and extinguish Indian title on the lands of the Cherokee, Chickasaw, Choctaw, Creek and Seminole nations.

It is important here to consider how tribes viewed President Andrew Jackson. In the war with the Creeks who had joined with the British, Jackson and Junaluska, A Cherokee leader born in western North Carolina was with him in Alabama during a meeting with a council of Creek Indians. One of the Creek Indians had a knife and started toward Jackson. Junaluska had observed this and tripped him so that he was never able to plant the knife into Jackson. [DNCR]. For that act of saving his life, Andrew Jackson upon becoming President committed the largest official act of Native American genocide to date, against the Cherokees and the other "five civilized tribes" as they were called when he ordered their removal and the long "trail of tears" walk to Indian Country. This order was contrary to the U.S. Supreme Court Ruling in the Cherokee cases that follow.

## Chapter 5.

## The Binding Nature of Treaties comes into Question in 1871

Crucial during this period was the end of treaty making power of the Executive Branch when the U.S. Congress passed an Act on March 3, 1871.[Statute] This gave all power over Indian Affairs to the U.S. Congress. No one has ever challenged the constitutionality of this statute, based on the diminishment of the President's Article II constitutional powers, and whether it is constitution remains a question. Congress delegated power to the Executive to determine who is an Indian tribe and the terms of recognition. So March 3, 1871 marks the end of treatymaking power for the President with tribes.

A case, *Two Hundred and Seven Half-Pound Papers of Smoking Tobacco, etc., Elias C,. Boudinot et al., vs. United States*, 78 U.S. 616 (1871), resulted in determining that parts of a treaty, in this case the Cherokee Treaty of 1866, could be extinguished by the court, without the consent of the Cherokee people. The provision at issue in the treaty was article 10, that Cherokee citizens had the right to sell any product or merchandise without, "any tax thereon which is now or may be levied by the United States."

The Cherokee people had been removed under the leadership of President Andrew Jackson, to Oklahoma where they were forced to start their Nation, anew. Elias Boudinot, with his uncle, negotiated the purchase of tobacco manufacturing facilities in Missouri, which he moved to the Cherokee Nation in order to avoid the payment of taxes on the merchandise, where the products were tax-exempt according to the Cherokee Treaty of 1866. The court reasoned that domestic revenue laws would control, rather than the Treaty. Treaty making power had been ended only two months earlier, leaving the power and reliance on all Treaties, in question.

The court held that Indians could be taxed for businesses that they had on their reservation lands, although they had no representation in Congress and could not have representation, because they were not American citizens.

The federal government seized all of the tobacco and manufacturing equipment, leaving Elias Boudinot, his uncle and his tribe in financial ruin. In 1883, he sought recovery through the federal Court of Claims, a court of specific jurisdiction for claims of money against the federal government, asking for $175,000 and received $3,272.25. [See David Wilkins, *American Indian Sovereignty and the United States Supreme Court*, Univ of Texas Press (1997) pp.54-63]

## The End of the Treatymaking Era

From the earliest days of colonization in the 1500s until 1871, leaders and the President of the United States were empowered to make treaties with Native Nations. They may have been one-sided but at least there was a respect for Native Nations as parties to a government to government treaty. Then the government to government relationship was changed forever with the Indian Appropriations Act of 1871 that removed the power of the President to make treaties with Indian Tribes. The U.S. Constitution, however, gives the President that power:

> *Art. VI, Clause 2. He shall have Power, by and*

> *with the Advice and Consent of the Senate, to make Treaties, provided two thirds of the Senators present concur;* [U.S. Const., Art. VI, Cl. 2]

With the passage of the 1871 Act, Congress declared that *no Indian nation or tribe within the United States would be recognized as an independent nation with which the United States may contract by treaty.*[Appropriations Act].

This statute should have been challenged and found unconstitutional as a violation of the separation of powers doctrine. The separation of powers doctrine ensures a checks and balances system where each of the three branches of government have particular duties outlined in Arts. I, II and III of the U.S. Constitution.

Using an originalist analysis, making treaties with Indian Tribes was a priority for the Department of War in order to settle wars and conflicts over land and expansion under the "Manifest Destiny" doctrine. When the drafters of the Constitution wrote that they were undoubtedly acquainted with this major undertaking with the U.S. Indian Tribes. In fact, the process outlined in Art. VI, Clause 2 of the Constitution was followed, having Indian treaties ratified by Congress.

The first U.S. Supreme Court, with Chief Justice John Marshall confirmed this clause applies to treaties with Indians, holding that

> *"The Constitution, by declaring treaties already made, as well as those to be made, to be the supreme law of the land, had adopted and sanctioned the previous treaties with the Indian nations, and consequently admits their rank among those powers who are capable*

*of making treaties. The words 'treaty' and 'nation' are words of our own language, selected in our diplomatic and legislative proceedings, by ourselves, having each a definite and well understood meaning. We have applied them to Indians, as we have applied them to the other nations of the earth. They are applied to all in the same sense."* *Worcester v. Georgia*, 31 U.S. (6 Pet.) 558 (1832).

The constitutional Presidential power to make treaties with the Indian tribes was demonstrated to be coextensive with the power to make treaties with foreign nations, in cases in 1872, 1876 and 1908. [Holden, et. al.]. So it is clear that the treaty clause applies to Indian Nations.

Yet, in 1871, in an otherwise routine Indian Appropriations Act, the U.S. Congress put an end to the President's power to make treaties with Indian Nations. The Act further said that Indian Tribes were no longer "independent nations" so they were no longer to have treaties.

**Why 1871?**

The United States had categorized Indian Tribes by placing Indian Affairs in the U.S. Department of War, up until the establishment of the U.S. Department of Interior in 1849.6 This signaled a shift in Indian Policy to one where the U.S. would act as trustee rather than as enemy or conqueror. But the official declaration for the end of war with Native Nations happened in 1871.

Treaties were seen as bargaining chips to end war with Tribes and in exchange for an end to attacks and raids, Native Nations were given hunting and fishing rights and a place to live with boundaries to exclude others — reservation lands. With the end of war, the end of treaty making was the logical next step in the mind of legislators. Yet, it was an Art. II power, not an Art. I power.

The costs of Indian Wars and Treaties were both high, and Congress wanted to do away with it. They attempted to that with the 1871 Act. However, the wars did not stop. In 1881, the U.S. Army was debating whether they could execute three Apache Scouts who were part of the U.S. Army for mutiny without permission of the President. If they were still at war, they did not have to get the President's permission, but if there was a declaration of the end of war with Tribes, then they had to get the President's permission. They ended up asking permission and it was granted.7 As late as 1890, the Massacre of Wounded Knee was the result of the U.S. Army shooting and killing as many as 150 children and elderly Sioux in a pointless massacre out of fear of a brewing discontent among the Sioux. The resistance by the Plains Indian Tribes raged through the end of the 19th Century. In 1911 a massacre of four Cheyenne people by ranchers occurred in Nevada. And in January 1918, at Bear Valley, in southern Arizona, The Battle of Bear Valley was fought.

**So who would challenge the constitutionality of this statute?**

The end of treatymaking did not affect Indian Tribes with treaties. It only affected Tribes without treaties, and in 1871, that could mean Native Nations in most of California, Arizona and all points west. These Native Nations likely did not plan on treaties, typically seen as a cease fire agreement. They likely planned on living free and independent as they always had, unaware of the certainty of the flow of Manifest

Destiny that would soon claim all of their homelands. Only Indian Tribes in the process of negotiating a treaty would have seen an end to treatymaking and had a controversy. Perhaps they would have been happy to end the negotiations and it appears there are no examples of this happening. A "case or controversy" [U.S. Const., Art. III, Sec. 2, Cl. 1] is required by the constitution to enter the judicial system of resolution.

The Executive Branch is the party having its Art. II powers reduced and so should be the party to challenge this Legislative Branch action that is a violation of the Separation of Powers doctrine. But it is the Judicial Branch that should resolve that Constitutional question and it is very likely the Judicial Branch may determine this to be a "political question" and not accept the case. Even if the Executive Branch was in favor of ending treat making power with the Tribes, allowing this action to diminish Art II powers was a a moment when the President should have objected.

So there was no formal mechanism for the President to sign peace treaties with Tribes, now, and it was left to Congress to enact specific statutes for any Tribe that was to be recognized after 1871. But it was likely thought they were seeing the end of Indians, because policies that followed like allotment, assimilation and termination attempted to complete that government goal.

It was not until the 1960s when federal policy turned toward self-governance and a reverse in efforts to terminate Indian Tribes that the Bureau of Indian Affairs was delegated the task of investigating whether a tribe was a "real" Indian tribe and could be recognized. This led to hundreds of tribes being recognized as long as they met the criteria which included a history of a relationship with the federal government, usually demonstrated with a treaty between the tribe and the federal government. Many tribes without this documentation were left unrecognized, by the federal government. But many states had their own recognition processes for tribes that were not recognized by the federal government or that wanted state recognition, too (Catawba Nation is a state recognized tribe in N.C.). State recognition was also recognition of existing sovereignty and self-governance, but did not come with the federal trust responsibility and federal resources and benefits.

The federal recognition "criteria" process governed by published regulations has been uneven, unpredictable and political, characterized by unfairness and lack of justice for many tribes. For example, until 2018, astonishingly, the tribe of Pocahontas was unrecognized by the federal government. Still, the tribes that were governed by Chief Seattle, the Duwamish and Suquamish tribes, have not been recognized by the federal government, despite decades of petitions.

Today, there exists a group of federally recognized tribes and state recognized tribes in the United States and some federal legislation may apply whether their status is state or federal recognition.

The federal recognition process has long been criticized for its paradoxical criteria. That is, Indian Tribes were told to stop speaking their own language and stop cultural dances ($18^{th}$ Century); but these are evidence of a continuity of governance and practice as a Tribe, and without these, recognition could be denied. Here is a political cartoon from Indian Country Today, January 31, 2001, with other examples of the criteria required for recognition that was once illegal or punishable by death or resulted in death.

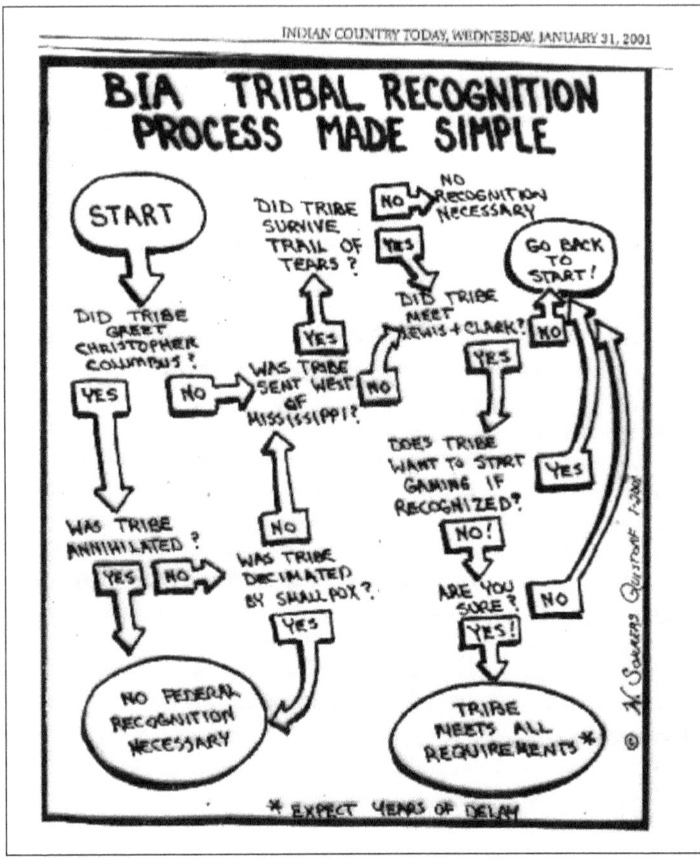
INDIAN COUNTRY TODAY, WEDNESDAY, JANUARY 31, 2001
BIA TRIBAL RECOGNITION PROCESS MADE SIMPLE
START
DID TRIBE GREET CHRISTOPHER COLUMBUS?
YES
NO
WAS TRIBE ANNIHILATED?
YES
NO
NO FEDERAL RECOGNITION NECESSARY
WAS TRIBE DECIMATED BY SMALLPOX?
YES
NO
WAS TRIBE SENT WEST OF MISSISSIPPI?
YES
NO
DID TRIBE SURVIVE TRAIL OF TEARS?
NO
NO RECOGNITION NECESSARY
YES
DID TRIBE MEET LEWIS + CLARK?
NO
GO BACK TO START!
YES
DOES TRIBE WANT TO START GAMING IF RECOGNIZED?
YES
NO!
ARE YOU SURE?
NO
YES!
TRIBE MEETS ALL REQUIREMENTS*
* EXPECT YEARS OF DELAY

## Chapter 6.

## The Rights and Status of Individual Indians

In 1879, a federal court addressed the question, whether an Indian is a person? In the case ***Standing Bear v. Crook*** (1879), a Nebraska federal court held that Indians are persons for the purpose of bringing a writ of habeas corpus to hear whether their freedom should be taken.

The gravity of such a decision was evident and the trial was watched very closely, because to find that an Indian was a "person" under the law, able to challenge their confinement, could challenge the entire reservation system.

The facts of the case are the following: Standing Bear and other Poncas, left their reservation and their tribal governments to become independent of their tribe. They moved to the Omaha reservation, and were arrested by the Army General Crook, acting upon orders of the Secretary of Interior, and detained until they could be removed back to their tribe and reservation. The District Attorney who was seeking their removal, argued that the court had no jurisdiction to hear their argument to challenge their confinement, because they were not American citizens, and only American citizens were entitled to file writs of habeas corpus. The court found otherwise, holding that any person is entitled to a writ of habeas corpus. The District Attorney further challenged that argument, citing the famous ***Dred Scott*** decision, which held that a slave could not challenge his confinement, even in a free state, because he was not a "person" under the law.

*The Omaha Daily Herald* editor, T. Tibbles, was outraged by the cruelty of confinement of Standing Bear and his group, so he used his position as editor to gain attention to their plight. Finally he sought the representation of John Lee Webster, a prominent attorney and A.J. Poppleton as co-counsel. The legal issues were presented at length, but particularly facts about whether the Indians were leading "civilized" lives, rather than what was considered the primitive lifestyle of Indians. With what were inordinately long arguments, Standing Bear's attorney, John Lee Webster, opened with a six-hour argument; the United States District Attorney, Lambertson gave a five hour argument; and Poppleton finished with a four hour argument. Then the court allowed Standing Bear to speak, and his remarks were interpreted for the court. It was recorded that Standing Bear rose, extended his hand toward the Judge's Bench, and for a long period of time, stood in that position, then spoke:

> *That hand is not the color of yours, but if I pierce it, I shall feel pain. If you pierce your hand, you also feel pain. The blood that will flow from mine will be the same color as yours . I am a man. God made us both.* . . [ after explaining that he wanted to return to the traditional Ponca homelands, he said:] *a man bars the passage . . . I . . .must obey his orders. If he says that I cannot pass, I cannot. The long struggle will have been in vain.* [After another long pause, he continues:] *You are that man.*[6]

Tibbles in the style of a reporter of the time, described the reaction in the court: the arresting Army

---

[6] James A. Lake, Sr., ***Standing Bear! Who?***, 60 Neb. L. Rev. 451, 476 (1981).

General Crook leaned forward and covered his eyes with his hands, women sobbed and tears appeared on the judge's face, then the entire courtroom shouted approval of the speech.[7] The opinion of Judge Dundy is excerpted, as he addresses the lengthy arguments of the parties.

---

## *United States ex. rel. Standing Bear v. Crook*

Case No. 14, 891 Circuit Court, D. Nebraska
25 F. Cas. 695 (1879)

District Judge Dundy.

During the fifteen years in which I have been engaged in administering the laws of my country, I have never been called upon to hear or decide a case that appealed so strongly to my sympathy as the one now under consideration. On the one side, we have a few of the remnants of a once numerous and powerful, but now weak, insignificant, unlettered, and generally despised race; on the other, we have the representative of one of the most powerful, most enlightened, and most Christianized nations of modern times. On the one side, we have the representatives of this wasted race coming into this national tribunal of ours, asking for justice and liberty to enable them to adopt our boasted civilization, and to pursue the arts of peace, which have made us great and happy as a nation; on the other side, we have this

---

[7] Id.

magnificent, if not magnanimous, government, resisting this application with the determination of sending these people back to the country which is to them less desirable than perpetual imprisonment in their own native land. But I think it is creditable to the heart and mind of the brave and distinguished officer who is made respondent herein to say that he has no sort of sympathy in the business in which he is forced by his position to bear a part so conspicuous; and, so far as I am individually concerned, I think it not improper to say that, If the strongest possible sympathy could give the relators title to freedom, they would have been restored to liberty the moment the arguments in their behalf were closed. No examination or further thought would then have been necessary or expedient. But in a country where liberty is regulated by law, something more satisfactory and enduring than mere sympathy must furnish and constitute the rule and basis of judicial action. It follows that this case must be examined and decided on principles of law, and that unless the relators are entitled to their discharge under the constitution or laws of the United States, or some treaty made pursuant thereto, they must be remanded to the custody of the officer who caused their arrest, to be returned to the Indian Territory, which they left without the consent of the government. On the 8th of April, 1879, the relators, Standing Bear and twenty-five others, during the session of the court held at that time at Lincoln, presented their petition, duly verified, praying for the allowance of a writ of habeas corpus and their final discharge from custody thereunder. The petition alleges, in substance, that the relators are Indians who have formerly belonged to the Ponca tribe of Indians, now located in the Indian Territory; that they had some time previously withdrawn from the tribe, and completely severed their tribal relations therewith, and had adopted the general habits of the whites, and were then endeavoring to maintain themselves by their own exertions, and without aid or assistance from the general government; that whilst they were thus engaged, and without being guilty of violating any of the laws of the United States, they were arrested and restrained of their liberty by order of the respondent, George Crook. The writ was issued and served on the respondent on the 8th day of April, and, the distance between the place where the writ was made returnable and the place where the relators were confined being more than twenty miles, ten days were allotted in which to make return.

On the 18th of April the writ was returned, and the authority for the arrest and detention is therein shown. The substance of the return to the writ, and the additional statement since filed, is that the relators are individual members of, and connected with, the Ponca tribe of Indians; that they had fled or escaped from a reservation situated some place within the limits of the Indian Territory -- had departed therefrom without permission from the government; and, at the request of the secretary of the interior, the general of the army had issued an order which required the respondent to arrest and return the relators to their tribe in the Indian Territory, and that, pursuant to the said order, he had caused the relators to be arrested on the Omaha Indian reservation, and that they were in his custody for the purpose of being returned to the Indian Territory. It is claimed upon the one side, and denied upon the other, that the relators had withdrawn and severed, for all time, their connection with the tribe to which they belonged; and upon this point alone was there any testimony produced by either party hereto. The other matters stated in the petition and the return to the writ are conceded to be true; so that the questions to be determined are purely questions of law. On the 8th of March, 1859, a treaty was made by the United States with the Ponca tribe of Indians, by which a certain tract of country, north of the Niobrara river and west of the Missouri, was set apart for the permanent home of the said Indians, in which the government agreed to protect them during their good behavior. But just when, or how, or why, or under what circumstances, the Indians left their reservation in Dakota and went to the Indian Territory, does not appear.

The district attorney very earnestly questions the jurisdiction of the court to issue the writ, and to hear and determine the case made herein, and has supported his theory with an argument of great ingenuity and much ability. But, nevertheless, I am of the opinion that his premises are erroneous, and his conclusions, therefore, wrong and unjust. The great respect I entertain for that officer, and the very able manner in which his views were presented, make it necessary for me to give somewhat at length the reasons which lead me to this conclusion.

The district attorney discussed at length the reasons which led to the origin of the writ of habeas corpus, and the character of the proceedings and practice in connection therewith in the parent country. It was claimed that the laws of the realm limited the right to sue out this writ to the free subjects of the kingdom, and that none others came within the benefits of such beneficent laws; and, reasoning from analogy, it is claimed that none but American citizens are entitled to sue out this high prerogative writ in any of the federal courts. I have not examined the English laws regulating the suing out of the writ, nor have I thought it necessary so to do. Of this I will only observe that if the laws of England are as they are claimed to be, they will appear at a disadvantage when compared with our own. This only proves that the laws of a limited monarchy are sometimes less wise and humane than the laws of our own republic -- that whilst the parliament of Great Britain was legislating in behalf of the favored few, the congress of the United States was legislating in behalf of all mankind who come within our jurisdiction.

Section 751 of the Revised Statutes declares that "the supreme court and the circuit and district courts shall have power to issue writs of habeas corpus." Section 752 confers the power to issue writs on the judges of said courts, within their jurisdiction, and declares this to be "for the purpose of inquiry into the cause of restraint of liberty." Section 753 restricts the power, limits the jurisdiction, and defines the cases where the writ may properly issue. That may be done under this section where the prisoner "is in custody under or by color of authority of the United States, . . . or is in custody for an act done or omitted in pursuance of a law of the United States, . . . or in custody in violation of the constitution or of a law or treaty of the United States." Thus, it will be seen that when a person is in custody or deprived of his liberty under color of authority of the United States, or in violation of the constitution or laws or treaties of the United States, the federal judges have jurisdiction, and the writ can properly issue.

. . . Now, it must be borne in mind that the habeas corpus act describes applicants for the writ as "persons," or "parties," who may be entitled thereto. It nowhere describes them as "citizens," nor is citizenship in any way or place made a qualification for suing out the writ, and, in the absence of express provision or necessary implication which would require the interpretation contended for by the district attorney, I should not feel justified in giving the words "person" and "party" such a narrow construction.

The most natural, and therefore most reasonable, way is to attach the same meaning to words and phrases when found in a statute that is attached to them when and where found in general use. If we do so in this instance, then the question cannot be open to serious doubt. Webster describes a person as "a living soul; a self-conscious being; a moral agent; especially a living human being; a man, woman, or child; an individual of the human race." This is comprehensive enough, it would seem, to include even an Indian. In defining certain generic terms, the first section of the Revised Statutes, declares that the word "person" includes co-partnerships and corporations. On the whole, it seems to me quite evident that the comprehensive language used in this section is intended to apply to all mankind -- as well the relators as the more favored white race. This will be doing no violence to language, or to the spirit or letter of the law, nor to the intention, as it is believed, of the law-making power of the government. I must hold, then, that Indians, and consequently the relators, are "persons," such as are described by and included within the laws before quoted. It is said, however, that this is the first instance on record in which an Indian has been permitted to sue out and maintain a writ of habeas corpus in a federal court, and therefore the court must be without jurisdiction in the premises. This is a non sequitur. I confess I do not know of another instance where this has been done, but I can also say that the occasion for it perhaps has never before been so great. It may be that the Indians think it wiser and better, in the end, to resort to this peaceful process than it would be to undertake the hopeless task of redressing their own alleged wrongs by force of arms.

Returning reason, and the sad experience of others similarly situated, have taught them the folly and madness of the arbitrament of the sword. They can readily see that any serious resistance on their part would be the signal for their utter extermination. Have they not, then, chosen the wiser part by resorting to the very tribunal erected by those they claim have wronged and oppressed them? This, however, is not the tribunal of their own choice, but it is the only one into which they can lawfully go for deliverance. It cannot, therefore, be fairly said that because no Indian ever before invoked the aid of this writ in a federal court, the rightful authority to issue it does not exist. Power and authority rightfully conferred do not necessarily cease to exist in consequence of long non-user. Though much time has elapsed, and many generations have passed away, since the passage of the original habeas corpus act, from which I have quoted, it will not do to say that these Indians cannot avail themselves of its beneficent provisions simply because none of their ancestors ever sought relief thereunder.

. . . The reasoning advanced in support of my views, leads me to conclude:

1. an Indian is a "person" within the meaning of the laws of the United States, and has, therefore, the right to sue out a writ of habeas corpus in a federal court, or before a federal judge, in all cases where he may be confined or in custody under color of authority of the United States, or where he is restrained of liberty in violation of the constitution or laws of the United States.

2. That General George Crook, the respondent, being commander of the military department of the Platte, has the custody of the relators, under color of authority of the United

States, and in violation of the laws thereof.
3. That no rightful authority exists for removing by force any of the relators to the Indian Territory, as the respondent has been directed to do.
4. That the Indians possess the inherent right of expatriation, as well as the more fortunate white race, and have the inalienable right to "life, liberty, and the pursuit of happiness," so long as they obey the laws and do not trespass on forbidden ground. And,
5. Being restrained of liberty under color of authority of the United States, and in violation of the laws thereof, the relators must be discharged from custody, and it is so ordered.

Ordered accordingly.

---

The court also opined that the expatriation statute to conclude that a Native American had a right to severe himself from his or her tribe forever. Because of this, the court held that the Army General was not authorized to remove Standing Bear and his group back to their tribe and reservation. The court held that they had jurisdiction to consider the writ of *habeas corpus*, and upon examination of the basis for their confinement, the court released Standing Bear and his group.

Unfortunately, perhaps given the new hope from this court's opinion on May 12, 1879; on May 13, 1879, Standing Bear's brother, Big Snake and 65 other Poncas left the Ponca reservation to visit the Cheyennes, although they had been denied permission from their federal Indian agent,

William Whiteman. Big Snake was arrested, and General Sherman authorized the arrest, writing, "The release under writ of habeas corpus of the Poncas in Nebraska does not apply to any other than that specific case." After several months of confinement, Big Snake was released and returned to the Ponca reservation, only to be arrested two months later, because Whiteman feared that Big Snake might assault him. On this basis Whiteman ordered Big Snake arrested and to be confined for the remainder of his life to Fort Reno, hundreds of miles away. When Big Snake resisted the arrest, a corporal shot him in the head using a rifle. [Lake, James A.]

In 1883, in a highly publicized murder trial, the ability of tribes to government themselves and mete out punishments for crimes of its members would be put on a political path of degradation and reduction of sovereign power.

In ***Ex Parte Crow Dog***, 109 U.S. 566 (1883), the families of the murdered Spotted Tail, and the family of Crow Dog, the murderer, met and in traditional fashion, discussed the terms of settlement and blankets and other gifts were given to the family of the victim.

A broad public outcry because of a resolution that failed to give Crow Dog the death penalty, resulted in a criminal trial. Although Spotted Tail was a favorite among the white community, Crow Dog won respect from the nation when he was released on bail, with a promise to appear for his trial. The federal agents arrested Crow Dog and took him to Deadwood, Dakota Territory, to the federal territorial court and he was tried and convicted by a federal jury.

Crow Dog convinced the marshall that he should be released to settle his affairs, and so he was released on the promise that he would return for sentencing. It was a snowy day when Crow Dog was due to report back to the Federal Marshall and all bets were that he would not appear; however out of the blizzard emerged Crow Dog, to the Federal Marshall's office at the appointed time. This was reported in the newspapers and Crow Dog was a hero. At this, volunteers appeared to file a writ of Habeas corpus on his behalf with the Supreme Court.

---

### *Ex Parte Crow Dog*

Supreme Court of the United States
109 U.S. 566 (1883)

Justice Matthews delivered the opinion of the court. The petitioner is in the custody of the marshal of the United States for the Territory of Dakota, imprisoned in the jail of Lawrence County, in the First Judicial District of that Territory, under sentence of death, adjudged against him by the district court for that district, to be carried into execution January 14th, 1884. That judgment was rendered upon a conviction for the murder of an Indian of the Brule Sioux band of the Sioux nation of Indians, by the name of Sin-ta-ge-le-Scka, or in English, Spotted Tail, the prisoner also being an Indian, of the same band and nation, and the homicide having occurred as alleged in the indictment, in the Indian country, within a place and district of country under the exclusive jurisdiction of the United States and within the said judicial district. The judgment was affirmed, on a writ of error, by the Supreme Court of the Territory. It is claimed on behalf of the prisoner that the crime charged against him, and of which he stands convicted, is not an offence under the laws of the United States; that the district court had no jurisdiction to try him, and that its judgment and sentence are void. He therefore prays for a writ of habeas corpus, that he may be delivered from an imprisonment which he asserts to be illegal.

The indictment is framed upon section 5339 of the Revised Statutes. That section is found in title LXX., on the subject of crimes against the United States, and in chapter three, which treats of crimes arising within the maritime and territorial jurisdiction of the United States. It provides that "every person who commits murder, . . . within any fort, arsenal, dock-yard, magazine, or in any other place or district of country under the exclusive jurisdiction of the United States, . . . shall suffer death. "Title XXVIII. of the Revised Statutes relates to Indians, and the sub-title of chapter four is, Government of Indian Country. It embraces many provisions regulating the subject of intercourse and trade with the Indians in the Indian country, and imposes penalties and punishments for various violations of them. Section 2142 provides for the punishment of assaults with deadly weapons and intent, by Indians upon white persons, and by white persons upon Indians. . .

SEC. 2145. Except as to crimes, the punishment of which is expressly provided for in this title, the general laws of the United States as to the punishment of crimes committed in any place within the sole and exclusive jurisdiction of the United States. . . shall extend to the Indian country.
SEC. 2146. The preceding section shall not be construed to extend to [crimes committed by one Indian against the person or property of another Indian, nor to] any Indian

committing any offence in the Indian country who has been punished by the local law of the tribe, or to any case where by treaty stipulations the exclusive jurisdiction over such offences is or may be secured to the Indian tribes respectively."

. . . .The first section of the Indian Intercourse Act of June 30th, 1834, 4 Stat. 729, defines the Indian country as follows: That all that part of the United States west of the Mississippi, and not within the States of Missouri and Louisiana, or the Territory of Arkansas, and, also, that part of the United States east of the Mississippi River, and not within any State to which the Indian title has not been extinguished, for the purposes of this act, be taken and be deemed to be the Indian country."

[T]he first article of the treaty of 1868, [states] that "if bad men among the Indians shall commit a wrong or depredation upon the person or property of any one, white, black, or Indian, subject to the authority of the United States and at peace therewith, the Indians herein named solemnly agree that they will, upon proof made to their agent and notice by him, deliver up the wrong-doer to the United States, to be tried and punished according to its laws."

But it is quite clear from the context that this does not cover the present case of an alleged wrong committed by one Indian upon the person of another of the same tribe. The provision must be construed with its counterpart, just preceding it, which provides for the punishment by the United States of any bad men among the whites, or among other people subject to their authority, who shall commit any wrong upon the person or property of the Indians. Here are two parties, among whom, respectively, there may be individuals guilty of a wrong against one of the other -- one is the party of whites and their allies, the other is the tribe of Indians with whom the treaty is made. In each case the guilty party is to be tried and punished by the United States, and in case the offender is one of the Indians who are parties to the treaty, the agreement is that he shall be delivered up. In case of refusal, deduction is to be made from the annuities payable to the tribe, for compensation to the injured person, a provision which points quite distinctly to the conclusion that the injured person cannot himself be one of the same tribe. Similar provisions for the extradition of criminals are to be found in most of the treaties with the Indian tribes, as far back, at least, as that concluded at Hopewell with the Cherokees, November 28th, 1785, 7 Stat. 18. The second of these provisions, that are supposed to justify the jurisdiction asserted in the present case, is the eighth article of the agreement, embodied in the act of 1877, in which it is declared:" And Congress shall, by appropriate legislation, secure to them an orderly government; they shall be subject to the laws of the United States, and each individual shall be protected in his rights of property, person, and life." It is equally clear, in our opinion, that the words can have no such effect as that claimed for them. The pledge to secure to these people, with whom the United States was contracting as a distinct political body, an orderly government, by appropriate legislation thereafter to be framed and enacted, necessarily implies, having regard to all the circumstances attending the transaction, that among the arts of civilized life, which it was the very purpose of all these arrangements to introduce and naturalize among them, was the highest and best of all, that of self-government, the regulation by themselves of their own domestic affairs, the maintenance of order and peace among their own members by the administration of their own laws and customs. They were nevertheless to be subject to the laws of the United States, not in the sense of citizens, but, as they had always been, as wards subject to a guardian; not as individuals, constituted members of the political community of the United States, with a voice in the selection of representatives and the framing of the laws, but as a dependent community who were in a state of pupilage, advancing from the condition of a savage tribe to that of a people who, through the discipline of labor and by education, it was hoped might become a self-supporting and self-governed society. The laws to which they were declared to be subject were the laws then existing, and which applied to them as Indians, and, of course, included the very statute under consideration, which excepted from the operation of the general laws of the United States, otherwise applicable, the very case of the prisoner. Declaring them subject to the laws made them so, if it effected any change in their situation, only in respect to laws in force and existing, and did not effect any change in the laws themselves. The phrase cannot, we think, have any more extensive meaning than an acknowledgment of their allegiance as Indians to the laws of the United States, made or to be made in the exercise of legislative authority over them as such. The corresponding obligation of protection on the part of the government is immediately connected with it, in the declaration that each individual shall be protected in his rights of property, person, and life; and that obligation was to be fulfilled by the enforcement of the laws then existing appropriate to these objects, and by that future appropriate legislation which was promised to secure to them an orderly government. The expressions contained in these clauses must be taken in connection with the entire scheme of the agreement as framed, including those parts not finally adopted, as throwing light on the meaning of the remainder; and looking at the purpose so clearly disclosed in that, of the removal of the whole body of the Sioux nation to the Indian Territory proper, which was not consented to, it is manifest that the provisions had reference to their establishment as a people upon a defined reservation as a permanent home, who were to be urged, as far as it could successfully be done, into the practice of agriculture, and whose children were to be taught the arts and industry of civilized life, and that it was no part of the design to treat the individuals as separately responsible and amenable, in all their personal and domestic relations with each other, to the general laws of the United States, outside of those which were enacted expressly with reference to them as members of an Indian tribe.

. . . offences committed by Indians against white persons and by white persons against Indians were specifically enumerated and defined, and those by Indians against each other were left to be dealt with by each tribe for itself, according to its local customs. The policy of the government in that respect has been uniform. . .

To give to the clauses in the treaty of 1868 and the agreement of 1877 effect, so as to uphold the jurisdiction exercised in this case, would be to reverse in this instance the general policy of the government towards the Indians, as declared in many statutes and treaties, and recognized in many decisions of this court, from the beginning to the present time. To justify such a departure, in such a case, requires a clear expression of the intention of Congress, and that we have not been able to find.

. . . It results that the First District Court of Dakota

was without jurisdiction to find or try the indictment against the prisoner, that the conviction and sentence are void, and that his imprisonment is illegal. The writs of habeas corpus and certiorari prayed for will accordingly be issued.

---

Crow Dog prevailed and was released from confinement and potentially the death penalty, but the case created the political will to pass the Major Crimes Act. The public outcry over this settlement, without the Anglo-American approach to trial and punishment for the crime of murder, led to the passage of the Major Crimes Act, which took self-government away from tribes when any of the major crimes were committed by Indians, even against other Indians.

The Major Crimes Act was passed as a rider to a general appropriations act which extended federal jurisdiction over all Indians for seven major crimes: murder, manslaughter, rape, assault with intent to kill, arson, burglary, and larceny. Questions over criminal jurisdiction continued to be raised in the courtroom over the next one hundred years.

---

In the next case, the U.S. Supreme Court addressed the question, whether an Indian is a citizen? In ***Elk v. Wilkins***, the U.S. Supreme Court in 1884 held that Indians are not citizens and therefore ineligible to vote, in a narrow reading of the Fifteenth Amendment, which granted the right to vote to all citizens. Justice Harlan had a strong dissent, finding that it was obvious that Indians were given citizenship if they had left their tribal nations, which was at least a beginning to recognition of full U.S. citizenship for Indians.

---

## *Elk v. Wilkins*

Supreme Court of the United States

112 U.S. 94 (1884)

[This is a petition asking for a review of the opinion from the U.S. District Court of Nebraska]

This is an action brought by an Indian, in the Circuit Court of the United States for the District of Nebraska, against the registrar of one of the wards of the city of Omaha, for refusing to register him as a qualified voter therein. The petition was as follows: "John Elk, plaintiff, complains of Charles Wilkins, defendant, and avers that the matter in dispute herein exceeds the sum of five hundred dollars, to wit, the sum of six thousand dollars, and that the matter in dispute herein arises under the Constitution and laws of the United States; and, for cause of action against the defendant, avers that he, the plaintiff, is an Indian, and was born within the United States; that more than one year prior to the grievances hereinafter complained of he had severed his tribal relation to the Indian tribes, and had fully and completely surrendered himself to the jurisdiction of the United States, and still so continues subject to the jurisdiction of the United States; and avers that, under and by virtue of the Fourteenth Amendment to the Constitution of the United States, he is a citizen of the United States, and entitled to the right and privilege of citizens of the United States. "That on the sixth day of April, 1880, there was held in the city of Omaha, (a city of the first class, incorporated under the general laws of the State of Nebraska providing for the incorporation of cities of the first class,) a general election for the election of members of the city council and other officers for said city. "That the defendant, Charles Wilkins, held the office of and acted as registrar in the fifth ward of said city, and that as said registrar it was the duty of such defendant to register the names of all persons entitled to exercise the elective franchise in said ward of said city at said general election. . . ."That on or about the fifth day of April, 1880, and prior to said election, this plaintiff presented himself to said Charles Wilkins, as such registrar, at his office, for the purpose of having his name registered as a qualified voter, as provided by law, and complied with all the provisions of the statutes in that regard, and claimed that, under the Fourteenth and Fifteenth Amendments to the Constitution of the United States, he was a citizen of the United States, and was entitled to exercise the elective franchise, regardless of his race and color; and that said Wilkins, designedly, corruptly, wilfully and maliciously, did then and there refuse to register this plaintiff, for the sole reason that the plaintiff was an Indian, and therefore not a citizen of the United States, and not, therefore, entitled to vote, and on account of his race and color, and with the wilful, malicious, corrupt and unlawful design to deprive this plaintiff of his right to vote at said election, and of his rights, and all other Indians of their rights, under said Fourteenth and Fifteenth Amendments to the Constitution of the United States, on account of his and their race and color. "That on the sixth day of April this plaintiff presented himself at the place of voting in said ward, and presented a ballot and requested the right to vote, where said Wilkins, who was then acting as one of the judges of said election in said ward, in further carrying out his wilful and malicious designs aforesaid, declared to the plaintiff and to the other election officers that the plaintiff was an Indian and not a citizen and not entitled to vote, and said judges and clerks of election refused to receive the vote of the plaintiff, for that he was not registered as required by law. "Plaintiff avers the fact to be that by reason of said wilful, unlawful, corrupt and malicious refusal of said defendant to register this plaintiff, as provided by law, he was deprived of his right to vote at said election, to his damage in the sum of $6,000. "Wherefore plaintiff prays judgment against defendant for $6,000, his damages, with costs of suit. "The defendant filed a general demurrer for the following causes: 1st. That the petition did not state facts sufficient to constitute a cause of action. 2d. That the court had no jurisdiction of the person of the defendant. 3d. That the court had no jurisdiction of the subject of the action. The demurrer was argued before Judge McCrary and Judge Dundy, and sustained; and the plaintiff electing to stand by his petition, judgment was rendered for the defendant, dismissing the petition with costs. The plaintiff sued out this writ of error.

. . . . The law upon the question before us has been well stated by Judge Deady in the District Court of the United States for the District of Oregon. In giving judgment against the plaintiff in a case resembling the case at bar, he said: "Being born a member of 'an independent political community' -- the Chinook -- he was not born subject to the jurisdiction of the United States -- not born in its allegiance." And in a later case he said: "But an Indian cannot make himself a citizen of the United States without the consent and cooperation of the government. The fact that he has abandoned his nomadic life or tribal relations, and adopted the habits and manners of civilized people, may be a good reason why he should be made a citizen of the United States, but does not of itself make him one. To be a citizen of the United States is a political privilege which no one, not born to, can assume without its consent in some form. The Indians in Oregon, not being born subject to the jurisdiction of the United States, were not born citizens thereof, and I am not aware of any law or treaty by which any of them have been made so since."

Upon the question whether any action of a State can confer rights of citizenship on Indians of a tribe still recognized by the United States as retaining its tribal existence, we need not, and do not, express an opinion, because the State of Nebraska is not shown to have taken any action affecting the condition of this plaintiff.

The plaintiff, not being a citizen of the United States under the Fourteenth Amendment of the Constitution, has been deprived of no right secured by the Fifteenth Amendment, and cannot maintain this action.

Judgment affirmed.

DISSENT

Justice Harlan and Justice Woods

. . . .Consequently, an averment that the plaintiff is a citizen and bona fide resident of Nebraska implies, in law, that he is subject to taxation, and is taxed, in that State. Further: The plaintiff has become so far incorporated with the mass of the people of Nebraska that, being, as the petition avers, a citizen and resident thereof, he constitutes a part of her militia. He may, being no longer a member of an Indian tribe, sue and be sued in her courts. And he is counted in every apportionment of representation in the legislature; the requirement of her

Constitution being, that "the legislature shall apportion the Senators and Representatives according to the number of inhabitants, excluding Indians not taxed and soldiers and officers of the United States army." Const. Neb., art. 3, § 1. . . . .By the act of April 9, 1866, entitled "An Act to protect all persons in the United States in their civil rights, and furnish means for their vindication" (14 Stat. 27), it is provided that "all persons born in the United States and not subject to any foreign power, excluding Indians not taxed, are hereby declared to be citizens of the United States." This, so far as we are aware, is the first general enactment making persons of the Indian race citizens of the United States. Numerous statutes and treaties previously provided for all the individual members of particular Indian tribes becoming, in certain contingencies, citizens of the United States. But the act of 1866 reached Indians not in tribal relations. Beyond question, by that act, national citizenship was conferred directly upon all persons in this country, of whatever race (excluding only "Indians not taxed"), who were born within the territorial limits of the United States, and were not subject to any foreign power. Surely everyone must admit that an Indian, residing in one of the States, and subject to taxation there, became, by force alone of the act of 1866, a citizen of the United States, although he may have been, when born, a member of a tribe. The exclusion of Indians not taxed evinced a purpose to include those subject to taxation in the State of their residence. Language could not express that purpose with more distinctness than does the act of 1866. . . . .

It was so interpreted by President Johnson, who, in his veto message, said: "By the first section of the bill all persons born in the United States, and not subject to any foreign power, excluding Indians not taxed, are declared to be citizens of the United States. This provision comprehends the Chinese of the Pacific States, Indians subject to taxation, the people called Gypsies, as well as the entire race designated as blacks, persons of color, Negroes, mulattoes, and persons of African blood. Every individual of those races, born in the United States, is, by the bill, made a citizen of the United States."

. . .

Born, therefore, in the territory under the dominion, and within the jurisdictional limits of the United States, plaintiff has acquired, as was his undoubted right, a residence in one of the States, with her consent, and is subject to taxation and to all other burdens imposed by her upon residents of every race. If he did not acquire national citizenship on abandoning his tribe and becoming, by residence in one of the States, subject to the complete jurisdiction of the United States, then the Fourteenth Amendment has wholly failed to accomplish, in respect of the Indian race, what, we think, was intended by it; and there is still in this country a despised and rejected class of persons, with no nationality whatever; who, born in our territory, owing no allegiance to any foreign power, and subject, as residents of the States, to all the burdens of government, are yet not members of any political community nor entitled to any of the rights, privileges, or immunities of citizens of the United States.

---

Native Americans were not granted the right of United States citizenship until 1924, although they may have been granted state citizenship as part of taking an allotment in the Allotment Act period.

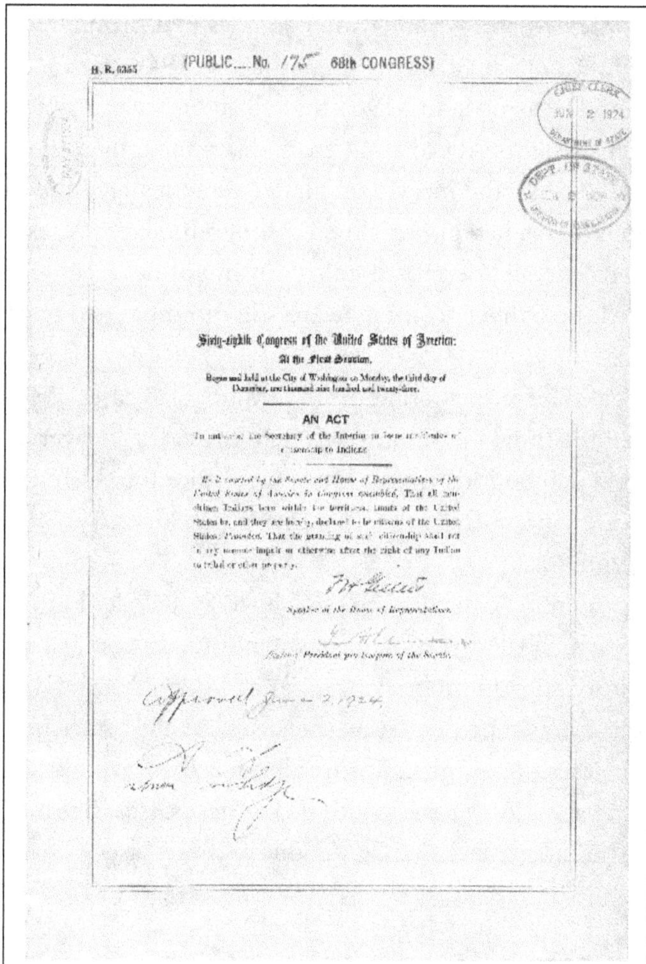
H. R. 6355 (PUBLIC No. 175 68th CONGRESS)

JUN 2 1924

Sixty-eighth Congress of the United States of America;

At the First Session,

Begun and held at the City of Washington on Monday, the third day of December, one thousand nine hundred and twenty-three.

AN ACT

To authorize the Secretary of the Interior to issue certificates of citizenship to Indians.

Be it enacted by the Senate and House of Representatives of the United States of America in Congress assembled, That all noncitizen Indians born within the territorial limits of the United States be, and they are hereby, declared to be citizens of the United States: Provided, That the granting of such citizenship shall not in any manner impair or otherwise affect the right of any Indian to tribal or other property.

Speaker of the House of Representatives.

Acting President pro tempore of the Senate.

Approved June 2, 1924.

The Act was passed December 1923 and signed by the President June 2, 1924, authorizing the Secretary of the Interior to issue certificates of citizenship to Native Americans. This Act did not distinguish between Indians who had left their tribes and those who remained with their tribes.

However, voting law is a state area of regulation and many states continued to refuse to allow Native Americans to vote. New Mexico and Arizona still had laws that prohibited Native Americans from voting as late as 1948.

It was not until 1965 that all states were prohibited by the Civil Rights Act of 1964 from discriminating against voters. Tribes and individual Native Americans in the eastern United States had already lived through the literacy tests that tried to ban all "people of color" from voting. Even if they passed the literacy test they were still often banned from voting.

The re-examining of the foundation cases in federal American Indian law approach here provides an overview of general perceptions from viewpoints other that historians who are writing from the documents produced by governments.

To look further into this history, a closer look shows that each tribal government has their own history, stories, religion and cultural practices that can be told through each of these eras represented by the cases. At the time of each of these cases, many tribes were still not federal recognized and were not subject to the outcome of these cases, but might later be subject to the rules set out in these cases.

## Bibliography

**Chapter 1.**
Ablavsky, Gregory, Making Indians 'White': The Judicial Abolition of Native Slavery in Revolutionary Virginia and its Racial Legacy (May 3, 2011). University of Pennsylvania Law Review, Vol. 159, p. 1457, 2011, Available at SSRN: https://ssrn.com/abstract=1830592

Blackhawk, Ned, *The Rediscovery of America: Native Peoples and the Unmaking of US History (2023).*

Fisher, Linford D., "Why Shall Wee Have Peace to Bee Made Slaves": Indian Surrenderers During and After King Philip's War Available to Purchase, *Ethnohistory* (2017) 64 (1): 91–114. *https://doi.org/10.1215/00141801-3688391*

Gallay, Alan, *The Indian Slave Trade: The Rise of the English Empire in the American South, 1670-1717 (2003).*

Horn, James. *A Brave and Cunning Prince* (Basic Books, NY 2021) p. 172, 189.

Library of Virginia, "Shaping the Constitution" at https://edu.lva.virginia.gov/oc/stc/entries/freedom-suit-claiming-indian-descent-of-an-enslaved-family-1804

National Park Service at https://www.nps.gov/jame/learn/historyculture/tobacco-the-early-history-of-a-new-world-crop.htm

National Park Service at https://www.nps.gov/parkhistory/online_books/jame1/mor

etti-langholtz/chap4.htm.

Reséndez, Andrés, *The Other Slavery: The uncovered story of Indian enslavement in America (2017).*

St George's Crown Community Newspaper at https://www.stgeorgescrownnewspaper.com/single-post/2017/11/23/stdavid-s-islanders

**Chapter 2.**

Anaya, James S., Indigenous Peoples in International Law 2d ed. Oxford Press 2004.

**Chapter 3.**

Albert J. Beveridge, Albert J., *The Life of John Marshall in four volumes* (1916)].

**Chapter 4.**

N.C. Dept. of Natural and Cultural Resources (DNCR)at https://www.dncr.nc.gov/blog/2024/01/23/junaluska-ca-1779-1858-q-2

**Chapter 5.**

16 Stat. 566; Rev. Stat. § 2079, now contained in 25 U.S.C. § 71.

Appropriations Act of 1871 at https://coloradoencyclopedia.org/article/indian-appropriations-act-1871

Holden v. Joy, 84 U.S. (17 Wall.) 211, 242 (1872); United States v. Forty-Three Gallons of Whiskey, 93 U.S. 188, 192

(1876); Dick v. United States, 208 U.S. 340, 355–56 (1908).

**Chapter 6.**

Lake, James A., Sr., ***Standing Bear! Who?***, 60 Neb. L. Rev. 451, 492 ,fn 102 (1981).

www.ingramcontent.com/pod-product-compliance
Lightning Source LLC
LaVergne TN
LVHW022019200926
848481LV00007B/2453
* 9 7 8 1 7 3 6 4 7 4 3 3 4 *